Each

and

Her

Camino del Sol

A Latina and Latino Literary Series

Each and Her

Valerie Martínez

THE UNIVERSITY OF ARIZONA PRESS

TUCSON

The University of Arizona Press
© 2010 Valerie Martínez
All rights reserved

www.uapress.arizona.edu

Library of Congress Cataloging-in-Publication Data
appear on the last printed page of this book.

Publication of this book is made possible in part by the proceeds
of a permanent endowment created with the assistance of
a Challenge Grant from the National Endowment for the
Humanities, a federal agency.

15   14   13   12   11   10   6   5   4   3   2   1

para una

y todas

for Andrea Michelle Martínez

1959–2008

Nothing less than the most radical imagination

will carry us beyond this place

—Adrienne Rich

Since 1993, over 450 girls and women have been murdered in or near the cities of Juárez and Chihuahua, Mexico, along the U.S.–Mexico border. Some were students; many were workers in the maquiladoras. The murders are linked by evidence of torture, sexual violence, and mutilation. Many young women migrate from other areas of Mexico to border cities both for education and for work. Despite local and federal investigations, intermittent arrests, and an international awareness of the murders, they continue in what appears to be a higher rate than in previous years. According to press reports, 28 women and girls were murdered in Ciudad Juárez and the surrounding areas in 2004. The number was 58 in 2006 and 86 in 2008.

Each
and
Her

l .

in this way

      could she

2.

we sit up straight

eyes red-rimmed

after a spanking

in the restroom

of the Shangri-La

Chinese restaurant

Juárez 1966

whenever he tells this

Dad says *pitiful*

and he felt bad

3.

they pack what they have

travel north

from Durango

Sinaloa

Nuevo León

Coahuila

rivers of dots

on a migratory map

papá

hay muchos

empleos allí

4.

strange how

light snow gleams

out window right

no snow out left

commuters

gape and snore

around me

in this early morning

northern-bound

train

a cloud quilt hovers

above mesas

5.

between

a layer of tangerine

6.

between

the Mexican interior
and U.S. border

three thousand maquiladoras

more than a million workers
at fifty cents an hour

imagine!
bastante para todos nosotros

7.

Rivera's girl on her knees

sky-blue-bound shoulders

behind

his thick feet

enormous bale of calla lilies

lifted to her back

8.

I have wanted

waited to write
until the click
of the garage door
and he goes

enter the fray
viciously
with Keats

truth beauty

meticulous
highlighting
clipping
filing
the newspaper
gray matter

have to?
so soon after she's gone?

9.

1995—nineteen by September

1996—sixteen between April and November

1997—seventeen between the ages of 10 and 29

1998—thirty including

Jessica Martínez Morales

Rosalina Valor Vásquez

Eréndira Ivonne Ponce

raped

strangled

beaten

shot

burned

right breasts severed

left nipples bitten off

10.

the assembly line

call it a revolution

in commodity forms

11.

in the backyard

all six fail to thrive

pink spots

balling buds

botrytis cinerea

also known as

cane canker

flower blight

tending them as if my life

12.

"It Really Is Amazing How Many Different Enemies
Are Out There to Get Your Roses!"

13.

this way

14.

Ciudad Juárez sits at the front lines of globalization. By 1996, nearly 40 percent of Mexico's exports were generated by the maquiladora sector along the U.S.–Mexico border. From modest beginnings, the maqui labor force has grown to nearly a quarter-million workers in Juárez alone. Most plants are U.S. owned, and women constitute more than half the workforce.

Maquiladoras can be 100 percent foreign, enjoying exemption from Foreign Investment Law. On average, companies save as much as 75 percent on labor costs by operating in Mexico.

Juárez is also home to perhaps the largest drug-trafficking cartel in the world, supplying the largest drug-consuming nation in the world—the United States.

15.

at the checkpoint border crossing

Mother Father the six of us
body to body in the Chevy

trinkets blankets
wrought-iron fence pieces
bottles of Montezuma tequila

cheap

over the limit

in the back
wet-seamed to the seat
we blow on each others' backs
pass a Shasta bottleneck

you cradle and wave
your yellow and indigo
paper-flower bouquet

16.

years later

in the recovery room

veins still pulsing with valium

outside the dust-furious desert

you and each and her

somewhere near consciousness

       between us

you said

       something kindred

       umbilical

       numinous

17.

it was three years
Amalia cooked and cared for us
in the San Ildefonso house

amalia malia malia

all the way from Juárez

from griddle to oven rack
the stack of warm
and freckled tortillas

18.

perspiring

pushing out her cotton shift

her maternal

    considerable

        roundness

19.

mis hijas

¿por qué están peleando?

she's your sister

you have to protect her!

20.

According to fossil evidence, the rose is 35 million years old. Cultivation began about 3000 BCE, probably in China. During the Roman Empire, roses were grown extensively in the Middle East and used as confetti, tincture, and perfume. In the 1600s, royal families used roses or rose water as legal tender. Cultivated roses were introduced into Europe in the late eighteenth century. Josephine established an extensive collection at Chateau de Malmaison.

"These were repeat bloomers, making them unusual and of great interest to hybridizers, setting the stage for breeding work, particularly for hardiness and a long bloom season."

21.

the number of girls and women

working in the post-NAFTA

maquiladora industry

472,423

while they can be hired legally

at the age of 16, it is common

for these girl-women

to get false documents

start work at 12, 13, 14

22.

at Algodones

one snowflake slaps

the bus window

the drywall factory

chuffs out its

white smoke

whose hands repeatedly

lift drop turn pull down

the metal blades

across the aisle

I watch her head

dip and rise

dip rise dip

interminably

23.

Campestre Virreyes

January 23, 1993

thirteen-year-old

Alma Chavira Farel

the documented first

24.

Valentin Fuentes Ignacio Mejía

Vicente Guerrero Juan Gabriel

Avenida Carlos Amaya

the streets of Juárez

muscular lock and grid

on Avenida Lerdo

between Ignacio Mejía

and Avenida 16 de Septiembre

the bridal district

Handmade gowns 50% off!

25.

the bodice is corset-like, exquisite,

intricately adorned with tiny roses

stitched by little hands

the plant manager calls them

his beauty queens

26.

"nearly all of the victims were poor,
young, and slender, with dark flowing hair
and warm, reddish brown complexions"

27.

this

way

28.

I wake to exhaust smell
forehead numb on the window

at left the reservation unfolds
in pink hills new tract homes
gleaming yellow playground equipment

we dip into the canyon
where the orange flag
stiffens violently with wind

north toward the neon-trimmed
San Felipe Casino

past the parking lot
post–night shift

watching her wrestle with air
coat and uniform ripping away

pushing a path to her car

29.

on the road between
Cuatitlan and Tlatelolco

fifty-seven-year-old
Juan Diego

day laborer
maker of mats

meets the Blessed Mother
Virgin Mary
of Guadalupe

juanito-juan
dieguito
juantzin
my little son

30.

spills from his tilma

Castilian roses

says

    through me

    thorn and red petal

    believe this

31.

"... the first I encounter are the Sibyls, those women chosen by God to prophesy the principal mysteries of our faith ... a woman like Minerva, daughter of the first Jupiter and mistress over all the wisdom of Athens. I see a Polla Argentaria, who helped Lucan, her husband, write his epic Pharsalia. I see the daughter of the divine Tiresias, more learned than her father. I see Zenobia, Queen of the Palmyrans, as wise as she was valiant. An Arete, most learned daughter of Aristippus. A Nicostrata, framer of Latin verses and most erudite in Greek. An Aspasia of Miletus, who taught philosophy and rhetoric, and who was a teacher of the philosopher Pericles. An Hypatia, who taught astrology and studied many years in Alexandria. A Leontium, a Greek woman, who questioned the philosopher Theophrastus, and convinced him. A Jucia, a Corinna, a Cornelia; and, finally, a great throng of women deserving to be named, some as Greeks, some as muses, some as seers, for all were nothing more than learned women held and celebrated ..."

32.

Jessica Lizalde León (3.14.93)

Lorenza Isela González (4.25.94)

Erica García Morena (7.16.95)

Sonia Ivette Ramírez (8.10.96)

Juana Iñiguez Mares (10.23.97)

Perla Patricia Sáenz Díaz (2.19.98)

Bertha Luz Briones Palacios (8.2.99)

Amparo Guzman (4.2.00)

Gloría Rivas Martínez (10.28.01)

Lourdes Ivette Lucero Campos (1.19.02)

Miriam Soledad Sáenz Acosta (3.28.03)

33.

no two sisters more unlike than us

cheerleader
chubby recluse

the drag-down hair-pulling fights

at night

holding the wooden handles
of a jump rope

bed-to-bed

    hold tight you said

between us

34.

Amalia went back to Juárez

dirt floors
sheets for doors

Coca-Cola in small bottles
in wood crates stacked

bundles of tortillas and tamales
out the front window

pesos and dollar bills
crushed on the ledge

we say
proudly

two refrigerators

unlike anyone
in the neighborhood

35.

"What is a domesticated woman? A female of the species? The one explanation is as good as another. A woman is a woman. She only becomes a domestic, a wife, a chattel, a playboy bunny, a prostitute, or a human dictaphone in certain relations."

36.

a typical maqui work schedule

60 hours per week

typical daily wage—$8.29

weekly salary—$49.74

deduction for union dues—4%

net weekly pay—$47.74

typical shared rent or contribution

to family income—$45.71

amount left over per week

for food clothes shoes

and medical attention—$2.03

37.

after the late shift

on the maqui bus

we stitch ourselves

one to another

take the middle seats

no decimos nada

y no miramos

nos nos cosemos

38.

some job applications ask women

if they are pregnant or sexually active

and

if so

what kind of contraceptives they use

and when they last menstruated

some workers are turned away

for being as little as three minutes late

begin and end their night shifts

without security or protective assistance

39.

the missive

from the attorney general

of the state of Chihuahua

You, Parents,

for raising up daughters

whose conduct does not conform

to the moral order

40.

"After all, it's very hard to go out in the street when it's raining and not get wet."

41.

July in central Juárez

the station wagon quits
every third block

Amalia Mother haggle with the men
for an engine fix

stay in the car and lock the doors

we huddle tight

sister-blouses damp
in the heat

crush of men
fingers through the window cracks

their smears on the glass

42.

is there no way

to avoid the clichés

woman-flower

man-monger

fear-fever-control?

43.

in the desert of Lote Bravo

two teenage boys

and their dogs

follow a trail

in scraps

of women's clothes

44.

Flor Márquez Valenzuela, 15

Airis Estrella Enriquez, 7

Dalia Noemí Diaz Montezuma, 16

Violeta Mabel Alvídrez, 18

Lilia Reyes Espinosa, 26

Verónica Berenice Gomez Amesquita, 19

Deisy Salcido Rueda, 26

Rosa Isela de la Cruz Madrigal, 19

Rosa Isela Corona Santos, 16

Rosa Isela Tena Quintanilla, 14

Rosa Linda Gardea Sandoval, 30

Rosa M. Arellanes García, 24

Rosa M. Placios Briones, 62

Rosa María González, 42

Rosa María Lerma Hernández, 23

Rosa Rivera Barajas, 36

Rosa Virginia Hernández Cano, 31

45.

". . . the best way to manage the disease is by inspection and
sanitation. Remove faded or blighted flowers, blighted leaves, or
entire plants infected at the base."

46.

out of snow dust

and winter brown

the serpentine

Rio Grande

rectangular squat

of Budaghers bar

where

trying to leave

he pulled his fist back

slammed it into

your face

47.

A single mass murderer

Copycat homicides

Two or three serial killers

Maqui bus drivers—five called "los choferes"

Members of a satanic cult

Organ harvesters

Federal agents and police officers

Killing parties linked to the drug cartels

more than fifty suspects in custody

with no effect on the murder activity

48.

Aphids: tiny pear-shaped insects that suck plant juices, preferring new growth

Beetles: hard-shelled insects that feed mostly on leaves and flowers

Borers: beetle or moth larvae that bore into cane

Downy mildew: a fungus appearing as white to grayish fuzz on the undersides of leaves

49.

"Sometimes, when you cross a shipment of drugs to the United States, adrenaline is so high that you want to celebrate by killing women!"

50.

sígame

51.

February 27

Carefully cut away the infected plant parts then pruned four of six bushes
according to instructions.

May 5

One, un-pruned, barely survives. Another produces healthy leaves but no flowers. Two, well-pruned, flower abundantly in quick wilting roses. Two, also well-pruned, bloom and bloom, keep blooming, relentless.

With proper care your rosebushes will enjoy four, even five, blooming cycles—keep cutting; keep them blooming!

52.

Julia Caldera would not believe that her daughter, María Elena, had been murdered. For four years she held to the belief that a rich man from the United States had fallen in love with María, taken her across the international border, and given her a much better life.

53.

in the first instance

a prelude

to multiple scenes

in hospital rooms

you sleep drugged and drunk

on Highway 64 a quarter mile

past the Taos Gorge Bridge

your plans to leap foiled

by a cocktail of vodka and Prozac

54.

in the third

you step into a moving car

concussion broken collarbone
lacerated liver right leg
shattered in three places

I hold to the railings of the bed
knuckles blue white

willing my legs
to stay solid

no sígame

56.

July 10

I dream rose vines shouldered by women in a ship's hold. Like those quinqereme drawings—Romans in rows, heaving their giant oars. Vines studded with dollar bills and Mexican coins. Pricks on their necks like stigmata. Through the apertures, not ocean but desert, a riverbed utterly dry.

July 11

I tend the barren rosebush, crushed by a tangle of grape vines. I cut away the clinging tendrils, choking leaves, dead gray canes. Little left but a huddled knot.

July 29

In the cool dark I find it: one new cane, caterpillar-green, stunned with two pale-pink blooms.

I refuse

58.

the bus hums into first gear

valley to mesa going red
to shale to purple rock

I tick off the landmarks

Algodones San Felipe
Budaghers Santo Domingo
the ramp to Cochiti Lake

one hour to work
another back
late in the day dark

crushed hair
shoes slipping off

59.

knowing them

only like this

6V.

"... and CHRIST proceeded forth from the Virgin Mary, as Adam had from the earth: Adam by the inbreathing of the Spirit of God—And breathed into him the breath of life;—and Christ by the coming of the Holy Spirit—the Holy Spirit shall come upon thee—was said of the Virgin Mary.

"But Christ also proceeded forth accordingly to the likeness of Eve: thus Eve came forth from a father without a mother ('from the rib'), so Christ came forth from a mother without a father (she 'knew not a husband'). Just as the first Adam brought forth from Eve without the participation of a woman, so Mary brought forth Christ without the participation of a man.

"The means whereby Eve and Christ came into being are identical: both received human nature by the power of God from one sex. At first the woman (Eve) did so from a man, and thereafter the man (Christ) did so from a woman.

"For this reason as Adam said of Eve so can we say of Mary, and through her even of Christ: This is now bone of my bones, and flesh of my flesh."

6l.

María Agustina Hernández

María Ascensión Aparicio Salazar

María Cendejas Martínez

María Clara Mavie Torres Castillo

María D. Quiñónez Corral

María de J. Barrón Rodríguez

María de Jesús González Apodaca

María de Jesús Lechuga Meza

María de Jesús Fong Valenzuela

María de la Luz Murgado Larrea

María de León Calamaco

María de los Angeles Acosta Ramírez

María de los Angeles Alvarado Soto

María de los Angeles Deras

María de Lourdes Galván Juárez

María de Lourdes Villaseñor

María del Refugio Núñez Lopez

María del Rocío Cordero Esquivel

María del Rosario Lara Loya, alias "La Burra"

María del Rosario Ríos

María Díaz Díaz

María Domitila Torres Nava

María E. Acosta Armendáriz

María Elba Chávez Caldera

María Elena Chávez Caldera

María Elena Salcedo Meraz

María Elsa Cano Gutiérrez

María Enfield de Martínez

María Estela Martínez Valdez

María Esther López de Ruiz

María Estrellan Cuevas Cuevas

María Eugenia Martínez Hoo

María Eugenia Mendoza Arias

María G. Rivas Triana Ramírez

María I. Chávez Martínez González

María Isabel Haro Prado

María Irma Blancarte Lugo

María Inés Ozuna Aguirre

María Isabel Nava Vázquez

María Isela Rivera Núñez

María Luisa Luna Vera

María Luisa Carsoli Berumen

María L. Gutiérrez

María Liliana Acosta Acosta

María Lopez Torres

María Luisa Cuéllar or María Luisa Estrada

María Maura Carmona Zamora

María Marisol Franco de García

María Máynez Sustaita

María Montes Lazcano

María Moreno Galaviz

María Cecilia Navarrete Reyes

María Osuna Aguirre

María Cristina Quezada Amador

María Rosa León Ramos

María S. Luján Mendoza

María Santos Ramírez Vega

María Santos Rangel Flores

María Saturnina de León

María T. Contreras Hernández

María Teresa Renteria Salazar

María Teresa Araiza Hernández

María Teresa Tullius

María Verónica Santillanes Nájara

62.

the bedroom

scatter of pills

stone-curled clutch of your palm

63.

64.

"'What is it?' I asked, for I was still afraid.

'It is the presence of the river,' Última answered.

"I held my breath and looked at the giant gnarled cottonwood trees. . . . Somewhere a bird cried, and up on the hill the tinkling sound of a cowbell rang. The presence was immense, lifeless, yet throbbing with its secret message."

65.

"He who is someone's thorn, he who is someone's prickle, he who is someone's fragment, he who is someone's shard, he who has someone's blood, he who has someone's red ink, he who has someone's legs, he who is someone's chips, he who is someone's slivers, he who is someone's eyebrows, he who is someone's beard, he who is someone's buttocks, he who has someone's quetzal feather plumage, he who has someone's heels, he who has someone's bits, he who has someone's pieces, he who has kinsmen, he who has second kin, he who has third kin, he who has kinsfolk, he who has another's liver, he who has another's entrails, all who came out of someone's belly, someone's throat."

66.

crush of the crowded Juárez market

Malia is first
hand clutching mine
Grandmother behind
tethered to Mom
Andrea Renée

grip so tight

I think I feel my finger bones break

67.

Graciela Iturbide's "Nuestra Señora de las Iguanas, Juchitan"

wears a crown of many large, live iguanas—a steely gaze—

68.

—maternal

    considerable

        roundness—

69.

—The Bacabs, immense iguanas, each sit at a corner
of the world, and hold up the sky—

70.

—Creator-Gods, each with a parietal

third eye, they represent the repeated attempt—

after many, many failures—

71.

—rosa ruidosa

continua

rosa espina de la boca—

72.

—to remake the world.

Notes

Dedication
Excerpt from "Motherhood: The Contemporary Emergency and the Quantum Leap," from *On Lies, Secrets, and Silence: Selected Prose, 1966-1978*, by Adrienne Rich. Copyright © 1979 by W.W. Norton & Company. Used by permission of the author and W.W. Norton & Company, Inc.

7
Diego Rivera, "El Vendedor de Alcatraces."

8
Lines 8 and 9 refer to Keats's "Ode to a Grecian Urn."

9
The most current and comprehensive list of names and dates of the murdered and disappeared women of Juárez can be found at http://womenofjuarez.egenerica.com/content/view/36/2/ (accessed November 2, 2009).

12
"Roses," http://www.rose-roses.com/problems/pests.html (accessed November 3, 2009).

14
Facts drawn from "Made in Mexico" (Maquiladora Management Services), www.Madeinmexicoinc.com/FAQs.htm (accessed November 3, 2009) and "The Other Side of the Ciudad Juárez Femicide Story," by Kathleen Staudt and Howard Campbell, *ReVista, The Harvard Review of Latin America*, Winter 2008, David Rockefeller Center for Latin American Studies at Harvard University, www.drclas.harvard.edu/revista/articles/view/1034 (accessed November 3, 2009).

20

The second section paraphrases information in "The History of Roses" by Greg Stack, www.urbanext.uiuc.edu (accessed November 3, 2009).

21

This section and section 37 quote various facts in "Maquiladoras at a Glance," CorpWatch, 6/30/1999, www.corpwatch.org (accessed November 3, 2009).

26

31

The quote is from Sor Juana Inés de la Cruz. Margaret Sayers Peden's translation of "La Respuesta a Sor Filotea," the first translation of the work into the English language, was originally commissioned by a small independent press, Lime Rock Press, Inc., Salibury, CT. It appeared in 1982 in a limited edition entitled *A Woman of Genius: The Intellectual Biography of Sor Juana Inés de la Cruz*, with photographs by Gabriel North Seymour. Copyright ©1982 by Lime Rock Press, Inc. Reprinted by permission.

35

38
"Some workers are turned away / for being as little as three minutes late / begin and end their night shifts / without security or protective assistance." Celeste Kostopulos-Cooperman, excerpt from the "Preface" to Marjorie Agosín, *Secrets in the Sand: The Young Women of Juárez.* Copyright © 2006 by Celeste Kostopulos-Cooperman. Reprinted by permission of White Pine Press (www.whitepine.org).

39 and 40
Stanza two paraphrases and section 40 quotes Debbie Nathan, "The Juárez murders: Sexism, corporate greed, and drug trafficking make Juárez a deadly town for Mexico's women. Hundreds are dead, but the killers remain free." *Amnesty Magazine,* http://www.amnestyusa.org/amnestynow/juarez.html (accessed November 3, 2009).

45
Information gleaned from "Botrytis Blight," (Plant Disease Diagnostic Clinic, Cornell University), http://plantclinic .cornell.edu/FactSheets/botrytis/botrytis_blight.htm (accessed November 3, 2009).

49
Teresa Rodriguez, citing a newspaper article quoting an "unidentified man," p. 256. Reprinted by permission of Atria Books, a division of Simon & Schuster, Inc., from *The Daughters of Juárez: A True Story of Serial Murder South of the Border,* by Teresa Rodriguez, Diana Montane, and Lisa Pulitzer. Copyright © 2007 by ROQ, Inc. All rights reserved.

52
Adapted from "Maria Elena Chavez Caldera: Biography," http:// www.answers.com/topic/maria-elena-chavez-caldera (accessed November 3, 2009).

60

Adapted from "Veneration of the Virgin Mary" in *The Shepherd*, by
Michael Polsky, Orthodox Christian Information Center, http://
www.orthodoxinfo.com/general/veneration_mary.aspx (accessed
November 3, 2009).

64

From *Bless Me, Ultima*, pp. 41–42. Copyright © Rudolfo Anaya
1974. Published by Warner Books Inc. 1994; originally published
by TQS Publications. Reprinted by permission of Susan Bergholz
Literary Services, New York, New York, and Lamy, New Mexico.
All rights reserved.

65

Excerpt from "The Manners of Speech of the Elders in Their
Ancient Orations," #5, in *A Scattering of Jades: Stories, Poems, and
Prayers of the Aztecs*," trans. Thelma D. Sullivan, ed. Timothy J.
Knab, The University of Arizona Press, 2003. Copyright © 2003
by the Balkin Agency, Inc. Used by permission.

67

The image is "Nuestra Señora de las Iguanas, Juchitan,"
photograph (1979), by Graciela Iturbide. Cover and frontispiece
from *Juchitan de las Mujeres*. Mexico: Ediciones Toledo, 1989.

69 and 70

Gleaned in part, from *The House of the Bacabs*, Copan, Honduras.
David Webster, editor; excavated under the auspices of the
Instituto Hondureño de Antropología e Historia. Washington,
D.C.: Dumbarton Oaks Research Library and Collection, *Studies
in Pre-Columbian Art and Archaeology*, no. 29, 1989, 73–81.

Acknowledgments

Grateful acknowledgment is made to the following publications where sections of *Each and Her* first appeared: *American Poetry Review, Mandorla, Breach Press*, and *Junta: Contemporary Latino/a Poetry of the Avant Garde.*

My deepest thanks to the following for their generous support and/or advice during the making of this book: Littleglobe, the Creative Writing and Literature Department of the College of Santa Fe, the Woodland Pattern Book Center, Society of the Muses of the Southwest (SOMOS), and The Institute for Latino Studies at Notre Dame; Patti Hartmann, Kristen Buckles, and the staff at the University of Arizona Press; Francisco Aragón, Brenda Cardenas, Teresa Dovalpage, David Gallegos, Gabe Gomez, Maurice Kilwein Guevara, Chris Jonas, Patrick Kelly, Elizabeth Lemons, Dana Levin, Shelle Sánchez, J. Michael Martínez, María Melendez, Jane Miller, Sawnie Morris, Amy Pence, Emmy Perez, Levi Romero, David Sánchez, Sue Stauffacher, Molly Sturges, and Roberto Tejada.

Thanks to my family for their unflagging support, for their tremendous beauty in the face of loss, and to Paul—for every thing, every day.

About the Author

Valerie Martínez is the author of *Absence, Luminescent; World To World; And They Called It Horizon;* and *A Flock of Scarlet Doves: Selected Translations of Uruguay's Delmira Agustini.* Martínez's poetry, translations, and essays have appeared widely in journals and magazines including *American Poetry Review, Parnassus, Puerto del Sol, The Notre Dame Review, Mandorla, Tiferet, The Latino Poetry Review,* and *AGNI.* Her poems have also appeared in various anthologies of contemporary poetry including *The Best American Poetry* (1996), *New American Poets—A Breadloaf Anthology, American Poetry—Next Generation, Touching the Fire—Fifteen Poets of Today's Latino Renaissance, Renaming Ecstasy—Latino Writings on the Sacred,* and *Junta—Contemporary Latino/a Poetry of the Avant Garde.* Martínez served as assistant editor of the anthology *Reinventing the Enemy's Language—Contemporary Writing by Native Women of North America* and an essay about Joy Harjo (along with poems by Harjo and Martínez) appears in the anthology *Efforts and Affections: Women Poets and Their Mentors.* An animated version of Valerie's poem "Bowl," from *World To World,* is featured in the *Poetry Everywhere* series (PBS/The Poetry Foundation). Valerie is Executive Director of Littleglobe, Inc., an artist-run nonprofit that collaborates with diverse communities on large-scale art and community dialogue projects. She has a BA from Vassar College and an MFA from the University of Arizona. She has taught at the University of Arizona, Ursinus College, New Mexico Highlands University, the University of New Mexico, the College of Santa Fe, and in the rural schools of Swaziland. She was the Poet Laureate of the City of Santa Fe for 2008–2010. For more information, visit Valerie's Web site at www.valeriemartinez.net.

Library of Congress Cataloging-in-Publication Data

Martínez, Valerie, 1961–

Each and her / Valerie Martínez.

    p. cm. — (Camino del sol)

ISBN 978-0-8165-2859-2 (pbk. : acid-free paper)

I. Title.

PS3563.A73345E22 2010

811'.54—dc22

                        2010000443